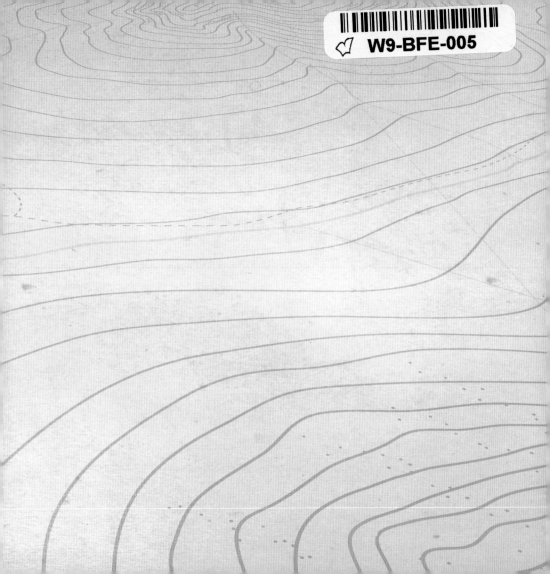

JOURNEY ON...

HOLY BIBLE

Never Alone

Emily Phoenix

The mission of CTA is
to glorify God by providing purposeful products
that lift up and encourage the body of Christ—
because we love him!

www.CTAinc.com

Journey On . . . Never Alone

Emily Phoenix
www.emilyphoenix.com

Copyright © 2015 CTA, Inc.
1625 Larkin Williams Rd.
Fenton, MO 63026

PRINTED IN THAILAND
ISBN: 978-1-940088-47-1

JOURNEY ON

To _____

. . . as your journey continues under the watchful care of your Father in heaven. May the Holy Spirit encourage you to live in love and joy—may he guide you in all your ways as you grow more and more like your Savior!

From _____

Date _____

Congratulations!

You graduated! What a triumph—after years of classes, tests, studies, your journey to graduation is finally over. You did it!

So how do you feel?

> a) Relieved?
> b) Excited?
> c) Nervous?
> d) *Terrified?*

. . . All of the above? . . .

Graduation is the celebration of the *end* of a journey: all of your hard work paid off, and you successfully reached this goal! But of course, it's also the *beginning* of a journey, perhaps a journey for which the directions aren't very clear.

Think about your new journey for a minute. Do you have a map? a guidebook? a companion to come along and read directions out loud? . . . Do you even have a destination in mind?

Whatever your feelings right now about reaching the conclusion of one adventure and embarking on another, God has this advice for you: "Don't be afraid, for I am with you. Don't be discouraged, for I am your God" (Isaiah 41:10). And in two weeks, or two months, or two years, as your fears and hopes and plans change—and change again? Well, then, God has this advice for you: "Don't be afraid, for I am with you. Don't be discouraged, for I am your God."

That's right. The same thing. And it's true.

You graduated! It's a huge accomplishment, and an exciting, probably slightly nerve-racking new beginning. But as your emotions about it change, and throughout the journey ahead, Jesus walks with you. He is with you.

Jesus Christ is the same yesterday, today, and forever.
Hebrews 13:8

Forever!

So you begin . . .

If you remain in me and my words remain in you,
you may ask for anything you want,
and it will be granted!
John 15:7

What lies behind you and what lies in front of you,
pales in comparison to what lies inside of you.
—Ralph Waldo Emerson

Journey:

The movement from

a) one place to another;
or
b) one phase to another
(even more exciting!)

The LORD your God is living among you.
He is a mighty savior.
He will take delight in you with gladness.
With his love, he will calm all your fears.
He will rejoice over you with joyful songs.
Zephaniah 3:17

The feeling remains that God is on the journey, too.
—Saint Teresa of Avila

List the 2 biggest celebrations in your life prior to your graduation.

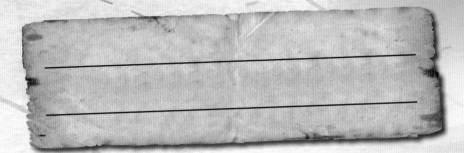

_____

_____

This is the day the LORD has made. We will rejoice and be glad in it.
Psalm 118:24

Celebrate!

Embrace the moment! Celebrate this milestone! Rejoice and be glad in your accomplishment! Classwork and assignments are done (for now), and it's time to revel in the experience.

So, how did you *get* here?? You've come this far because God has flooded your life with his blessings. Your heavenly Father has brought you to this day. His Word reminds you of his gift to you, more precious than sheet sets or picture frames or even graduation cards filled with cash: a living and personal relationship with your Savior, Jesus Christ. That relationship gives you all the strength you will need as you continue on your journey.

**Every day
is my favorite day.**

List 3 experiences you are looking forward to in the next few months of your life.

_____

_____

_____

The people who walk in darkness will see a great light.
For those who live in a land of deep darkness, a light will shine. . . .
The government will rest on his shoulders.
And he will be called: Wonderful Counselor, Mighty God,
Everlasting Father, Prince of Peace.
His government and its peace will never end.
Isaiah 9:2, 6–7

What's Next?

By now, you've heard the formula from teachers, counselors, guardians, coaches:

*First, you set a goal.

*Next, you formulate a plan for reaching that goal.

*Then, you work toward your goal, according to your plan.

*Finally, thanks to your efforts, you achieve your goal.

In reality, though, it's not quite like that, is it? In reality, no matter how desirable the goal, how clear the plan, or how hard you work to realize your dream, there is a *lot* of waiting. You can't start that great job until the company sends you the contract. You can't move into that new apartment until the previous tenant moves out. You can't attend those exciting new classes until the semester begins, and the professors are ready to teach. The truth is, sometimes looking forward to something is really all you can do—sometimes, you just have to wait.

Waiting. It's not always easy. Think, for example, about the expectation and anticipation believers held in their hearts for hundreds of years as they waited for the Savior to come into the world. Prophecies, like the one here from Isaiah 9, raised everyone's hopes. But it took 700 years for God's promise through Isaiah to come true!

There was certainly a lot to look forward to. But those who heard Isaiah's words back then had to learn to balance anticipation with living in the present. God urged his people to remain faithful as they waited and watched.

As you anticipate the next phase in your own journey, you, too, can live in the love God has shown for you. You might be chomping at the bit to take the next step, but your Lord encourages you to rely on his grace and live out his love as you wait.

Because, of course, God keeps his promises. What happened when that long-promised Savior finally arrived? Those who believed celebrated! They experienced the kind of joy and peace only God can give. What will happen as you take the next step in your journey? God will keep on fulfilling his promises to you. You will experience the kind of joy and peace that only God can give.

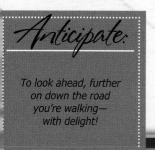

Anticipate.

To look ahead, further on down the road you're walking— with delight!

Fear

Is reality setting in yet? You are making significant changes in your life. It's really happening! You are leaving school and the people you see every day. You might find yourself in a new place or a new situation, alone. You are starting down a new path, and you're not quite sure what to expect. You might be thinking, "Will people like me? Will I like them? Will I be able to manage the workload? Will I miss my friends and family? What if I get sick? What if I make a mistake?" . . . So many fears.

You might try to hide your fears—or perhaps your fears make you want to hide *yourself*—but you can't hide from God. He created you uniquely, and he knows you better than you know yourself. He loves you no matter what, and he promises to stay right there with you always—every unnerving, uncertain, unanticipated minute of every day. He invites you to share your anxious thoughts with him. He longs for you to do that! He wants you to trust that he will take care of you, just as he has promised.

In fact, Jesus already took care of a huge source of fear: sin. He hoisted your burden onto his own shoulders, carried it all the way to the cross, and died so that you may live fearlessly and freely, enjoying all the other blessings God has given to you. So go ahead! You can boldly take the next step forward, knowing that God is with you—which means you have everything you will need to face your fear.

> *You made all the delicate, inner parts of my body*
> *and knit me together in my mother's womb.*
> *Thank you for making me so wonderfully complex!*
> *Your workmanship is marvelous—how well I know it.*
> *You watched me as I was being formed in utter seclusion,*
> *as I was woven together in the dark of the womb.*
> *You saw me before I was born.*
> *Every day of my life was recorded in your book.*
> *Every moment was laid out*
> *before a single day had passed.*
>
> *Psalm 139:13–16*

Don't be afraid, little flock. For it gives your Father great happiness to give you the Kingdom.
Luke 12:32

Possibilities

It's time to take the next step, and your excitement is building! Everything is new, new, new. New opportunities. New possibilities. New relationships.

Whatever your circumstances, you can live in the joy Jesus gives and share his love in your actions and through your words as you stride forward without hesitation. Jesus is the source of all true and lasting joy. Listen to what he says:

> *I have loved you even as the Father has loved me. Remain in my love. . . . I have told you these things so that you will be filled with my joy. Yes, your joy will overflow!*
> John 15:9, 11

You know the kind of love Jesus is talking about when he says, "Remain in my love." That's the love that bled and died for you on Calvary's cross! That love is all you need as you move forward and enjoy the excitement of each new step in your journey, each new chapter in your adventure.

New:
_____

a) Fresh;
b) unknown, uncharted; and
c) full of possibilities.

The only difference between *fear* and *excitement* is your attitude about it.
—Unknown

List 4 details of your daily routine that are changing as you continue your journey.

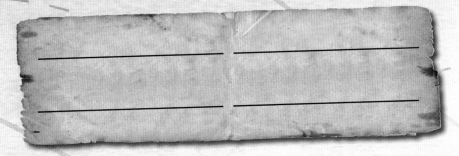

_____   _____

_____   _____

Jesus Christ is the same yesterday, today, and forever.
Hebrews 13:8

Transition

The transitions we make after major life events aren't always easy.
There are so many variables, so many unknowns. So much is in flux.
So many details need to be worked out.

God's people, the Israelites, experienced a life-changing transition
of their own. For 400 years, they and their parents and their
grandparents before them had lived as slaves under the rule of
Egypt's Pharaoh. Then, through Moses, the Lord delivered them from
slavery and led them through the desert on a forty-year journey to
the Promised Land.

The transition from slavery to freedom certainly shook up the
people's daily routine! But through it all, the Lord provided guidance,

✓ Friends
✓ Living situation
✓ Daily routines
✓ Transportation
✓ Food
✓ Weekend activitie

protection, and even the food and water they needed day to day as they continued their trek. (When was the last time you read this account of God's incredible promise and provision? Refresh your memory by turning to the Book of Exodus in the Bible, beginning with Chapter 12.)

God is with you, too, as you experience this life-changing transition—graduation. Through every change that lies ahead, your Lord will guide you. He will keep on meeting your every need. No matter what else changes, remember that your Savior's love for you will never change. His forgiveness, friendship, and peace are yours through every transition in life.

JOURNEY ON

What are 5 things that make you feel anxious?

_____ _____

_____ _____

_____

Anxiety

Graduation marks one of life's earliest and biggest transitions. It opens the door to new opportunities in school, work, and relationships. As that door opens, anxiety and stress often slip in, too.

You might be asking questions like . . .

Will my clothes be okay?

What if I miss something?

Will I get homesick?

Can I really afford this?

What if I'm not ready?

What if everybody is more fun than I am?

The Lord Jesus has one great answer to all your many questions:

I tell you not to worry about everyday life. . . . Your heavenly Father already knows all your needs. Seek the Kingdom of God above all else, and live righteously, and he will give you everything you need.
Matthew 6:25, 32–33

New situations come with new challenges. They hatch new batches of butterflies in almost everybody's stomach. Stress and failure, too, are part of life—everyone's life! But you don't have to deal with these feelings by yourself.

Jesus knows what you need. He's there for you. He wants to be the Friend to whom you run in times of stress, the first Friend you turn to when you're feeling anxious, the Friend on whom you most depend. In moments of angst, remembering your Savior's care for you will help you pull through. He loved you so much that he died for you! He won't abandon you just because you are jittery.

Trust your Savior to pick you up, comfort you, and give you the confidence you need to continue on your journey, taking each minute, each day as it comes.

Don't worry about anything; instead, pray about everything. Tell God what you need, and thank him for all he has done. Then you will experience God's peace, which exceeds anything we can understand. His peace will guard your hearts and minds as you live in Christ Jesus.
Philippians 4:6–7

List the names of the 6 people whose relationships are most important in your life right now.

————————— —————————

————————— —————————

————————— —————————

**A friend is someone who knows all about you—
but loves you just the same.**
—Unknown

New Relationships

Who knows you better than anyone else? Who can finish your sentences—and often does? Whose sentences can you finish? Who makes you laugh until you cry? If you had a big problem, whom would you call or text first? Is that person traveling with you to the next stop on your journey? Or do you have to part ways? You will stay in touch, of course, but perhaps both of you realize it's time to form new relationships.

In new settings, we naturally make new friends. This might be easy for you or hard, but either way, friends are important as we grow into life's new stages.

Consider David and Jonathan: best friends in a less-than-ideal situation. Jonathan's father was king and insanely jealous of David. Still, the friendship between these two young men endured. (You can read about their close bond in 1 Samuel 18:1–4.)

As you develop new relationships, you have the chance to model them after the one your Savior has developed with you. How does that one work again? Think about what Jesus does for you . . . He gives, without expecting anything in return. He listens and helps. He forgives.

How would your relationships change if you looked for ways to be like Jesus to those around you? How would your friendships grow differently if you thought about ways to talk about Jesus with your new friends? How could your journey through life be enriched if your companions encouraged you to face each adventure with faith?

Making Plans

You have your whole life in front of you. You have plans to make! Plans to set in motion! Working toward your goals gives you many opportunities for new experiences. Up to this point in your life, other people have made plans and set goals for you—now it's your turn!

Not all plans work out. Not all goals are achieved. (And that's not always a bad thing!) Your Lord does not promise that all your plans will work out, but he does guarantee that he wants what's best for you. He does guarantee that he will work in and through all that happens in your life for your ultimate good. And he guarantees that he will walk with you every step of the way.

The best plan for your life is the one that Jesus already fulfilled. He made the ultimate sacrifice for you, dying for your sins and rising again to defeat death so that you can live eternally.

So now, whatever you plan, plan to live in his love, sharing that love in all the plans you make.

> *Commit your actions to the LORD,*
> *and your plans will succeed. . . .*
> *We can make our plans,*
> *but the LORD determines our steps.*
> Proverbs 16:3, 9

> *Trust in the LORD with all your heart*
> *and lean not on your own understanding;*
> *in all your ways submit to him,*
> *and he will make your paths straight.*
> Proverbs 3:5–6 NIV®

JOURNEY ON

Growing Pains

It's such a simple song. It may be the first song you ever learned. You know the words, maybe to several verses.

Here's a challenge for you: can you apply this simple song to every single day, every single situation in your life? Try it today. Without Jesus' love, you are weak and helpless—but your Savior is strong! His love gives you the strength you need to endure life's challenges. The assurance that Jesus loves you can make the pains of change easier to bear.

Jesus loves me—this I know,
For the Bible tells me so;
Little ones to Him belong—
They are weak, but He is strong.

Yes, Jesus loves me!
Yes, Jesus loves me!
Yes, Jesus loves me!
The Bible tells me so.

—William Batchelder Bradbury

You may be on your own, making your own decisions, becoming more independent, making mistakes, and probably learning some things the hard way. Perhaps you have realized that you can't "do life" successfully on your own. Thank God, you don't have to! His grace and power are at work when you depend on Jesus and trust in what he has done and has promised to do for you. After all, Jesus says:

My grace is sufficient for you, for my power is made perfect in weakness.
2 Corinthians 12:9 NIV®

Weekends

Weekends are a time for rest. You've been going and going nonstop all week—now you can take a step back and relax. Remember, God rested after creating the universe:

> *God blessed the seventh day . . .*
> *because it was the day when he rested*
> *from all his work of creation.*
> Genesis 2:3

No, he wasn't tired. He was setting an example for us! Without really taking a break from all that you have going on, it will get harder and harder to *keep* going on.

So enjoy your weekend: sink into this time to rest. When your feet are up and your muscles are relaxing, thank God for the days he gives us to unplug and unwind. Thank him for the deep and constant comfort you have in the love of Jesus, your Savior.

And ask him to help you know that comfort all week long.

Weekend:

A two-day period when one can

a) sleep until noon;
b) socialize;
and
c) grow in faith.

What 8 things about school do you miss or expect to miss the most?

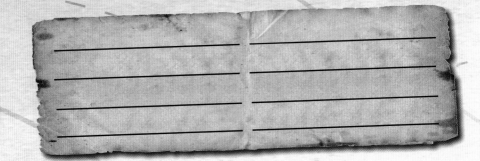

Longing for the Past

You want your old life back. You miss your friends and all the memories you made in school. Sometimes you just want to go back to the way things were. Your new experiences are tiring and stressful.

These feelings are natural—you're only human!—and challenging. But if there is one thing that is 100% guaranteed about every challenge, it's that your Savior-God has *not* left you to face it alone. He's there with you. He cares for you unconditionally and invites you to lean your full body-and-soul weight on his promises, like this one:

> *Even youths grow tired and weary,*
> *and young men stumble and fall;*
> *but those who hope in the Lord*
> *will renew their strength.*

They will soar on wings like eagles;
they will run and not grow weary,
they will walk and not be faint.
Isaiah 40:30–31 NIV®

When difficulties seem overwhelming, God is stronger. Your heavenly Father kept his promise to send a Savior for you. He will keep all his other promises to you, too. Let those faithful promises bolster your courage and keep you afloat.

It is only through labor and painful effort, by grim energy and resolute courage that we move on to better things.
—Theodore Roosevelt

Charged Up, Ready to Go

You are motivated.

You are on a good track in daily life and relationships.

You also want to keep growing in your faith and seeking new avenues of knowledge.

You learned about God and went to church as you grew up, but now you want to know so much more! Just as you are learning and growing in other ways, so you want to grow in faith and knowledge. God will provide the tools you need. Watch for them! And look for ways to share your faith; it's one way to grow up spiritually.

You must remain faithful to the things you have been taught.
You know they are true, for you know you can trust those who taught you.
You have been taught the holy Scriptures from childhood,
and they have given you the wisdom to receive the salvation
that comes by trusting in Christ Jesus.
All Scripture is inspired by God and is useful to teach us what is true
and to make us realize what is wrong in our lives.
It corrects us when we are wrong and teaches us to do what is right.
2 Timothy 3:14–16

An invincible determination can accomplish almost anything.
—Thomas Fuller

Diligence:

a) Consistent effort;
b) persistence;
and
b) Spirit-inspired resolve.

What *9* factors cause chaos in your life right now?

Be still, and know that I am God.
Psalm 46:10 NIV®

Chaos

Why does everything have to be so *loud*? Chaos makes it difficult to focus on the tasks at hand. Sometimes all we want is some peace and quiet. Is that too much to ask?

As the world around us shouts messages of pressure, sadness, and despair, our Lord whispers a different message altogether: *I love you. I have always loved you. I will always love you.* Listen! Even in the chaos, you can hear it.

Jesus entered our chaotic world. He experienced arguments, nonsense, and mocking. In it all, he kept on praying quietly for God's will to be done.

God's will *was* done, through Jesus' own death and resurrection. Let this truth live in your heart, providing an oasis of peace no matter how chaotic the circumstances around you grow.

Pace Yourself

Ever participated in a marathon or a 100-yard dash? Either way, you need a strategy, right?

The same thing is true for your journey through life. Whether it is long or short, you can count on this race being an adventure full of twists and turns. So here's a strategy for you to try:

*Keep your eyes focused on the cross of your Savior: it's a reminder that
  Jesus erased *your* sin with *his* death.
*Trust your Savior's promises. He always follows through on them. Turn to
  his Word when you feel unsure.
*Talk to God. He's listening! Ask him for courage, patience, a good night's sleep . . .
  He will give you what you need to continue on your journey.

*Don't you realize that in a race everyone runs, but only one person gets the prize?
So run to win! All athletes are disciplined in their training.
They do it to win a prize that will fade away, but we do it for an eternal prize.*
1 Corinthians 9:24–25

Whether life feels like a marathon or a bunch of short sprints, you still need to put one foot in front of the other.

List 10 prayer requests you have at this moment.

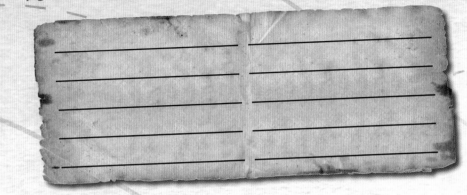

Stay in Conversation

Here's a question for you: what does it take to maintain relationships with friends?

a) Communication
b) Quality time together
c) Honesty
d) All of the above

If you chose d, you're right. And the same goes for your relationship with Jesus. You talk to him in prayer. He talks to you through his Word. You spend time with him. You're open and honest with him. You grow closer to each other.

David wrote many psalms as prayers of thanksgiving and joy, but he also sought guidance.

Jonah talked to God from the belly of the great fish—which must have been a very interesting backdrop for prayer!

Jesus talked to his heavenly Father consistently throughout his life. In constant communication, he sought to understand and do God's will in every situation.

Conversing with God about what challenges you, what you are thankful for, and everything in between will help keep you on the right path as you continue to journey forward. And you will be able to find comfort in remembering that your Friend Jesus—the One who cares so much about you—is right there beside you all the time.

Rejoice in our confident hope.
Be patient in trouble,
and keep on praying.
    Romans 12:12

Prayer is simply a
conversation with the
One who loves you most of all.

Loving Others

Jesus gave his followers two commandments:

> **"You must love the Lord your God with all your heart,**
> **all your soul, and all your mind."**
> **This is the first and greatest commandment.**
> **A second is equally important:**
> **"Love your neighbor as yourself."**
> Matthew 22:37-40

Only two commands. How hard can it be? If you've tried, you know the answer: *very!* It's not easy to give the Lord and other people priority in your heart and life. But it is what Jesus wants for you.

How thankful we are that Jesus died for all the times we act in sinful selfishness instead of loving generosity! How thankful we can be that Jesus' sacrifice on the cross makes our love for others possible! How could your thankfulness spill over into the way you interact with the people around you?

J. O. Y.

Jesus

Others

Yourself

Write down _11_ ways you can serve your neighbor.

Serving

Continuously throughout his ministry, Jesus modeled true, servant-like love. Often, he performed miracles. Perhaps even more often, he spent time with people considered of lesser value to society. Most significantly, Jesus sacrificed himself, giving up his life for us on the cross. On the night before that last, greatest act of service, Jesus demonstrated his love and servant heart by washing his disciples' feet. In doing so, Jesus did a task usually reserved for a lowly household slave. King of kings though he certainly was, Jesus showed his disciples true humility. He showed us what it means to serve one another. After he washed their feet, Jesus said to his followers:

> *Do you understand what I was doing?*
> *You call me "Teacher" and "Lord," and you are right,*
> *because that's what I am.*

And since I, your Lord and Teacher, have washed your feet,
you ought to wash each other's feet.
I have given you an example to follow.
Do as I have done to you.

John 13:12–15

Since Jesus is your Brother, your King, your Savior, and your Lord, you, too, are called to serve those around you. When you serve with a heart like Jesus' own heart, your service honors and glorifies God.

Say, What?

You have entered a new time of life, and it's time to speak up! You may be the youngest one in the crowd. You may still be finding your voice. That doesn't matter. You are important to your heavenly Father, and he wants you to be heard! You have something important to say. It matters!

In what you say, as in what you do, you can share Christ's love. Maybe your parents did that. Maybe your teachers and friends did that. If they did, they can tell you it's not always an easy task. It is always, though, a great opportunity when you get to witness to your Lord and to his promises, especially the promise he fulfilled by sending Jesus to be our Savior.

Knowing and trusting Jesus is a gift too wonderful for words, a gift so amazing that you will never fully understand it. But it is essential to share it with those who don't know God as their heavenly Father and Jesus as their very best Friend, the One who died for them.

As your journey through life continues, you will encounter many different kinds of new experiences. Pray especially for new opportunities to share Jesus' love. Then, *speak up!*

Don't let anyone think less of you because you are young.
Be an example to all believers in what you say,
in the way you live, in your love,
your faith, and your purity.
1 Timothy 4:12

Speak Up:

To voice your belief, even
when doing so is scary.

Write down _12_ dreams you have for your future.

Keep Dreaming

Something went wrong. Maybe one of your fears—of failure, rejection, hardship, or catastrophe—was realized. It's hard to keep on trusting God when disaster dashes your dreams. The plans you make won't always pan out as you had hoped. But your Lord and his love are bigger and greater than you could ever imagine. That love never ends, even when we can't explain the twists and turns in our individual lives.

It may be hard to see that right now. Disappointment is one of life's strongest emotions. Still, you don't have to let it be a game-changer. Think about what you have learned just now. Think about how to persevere, perhaps in another direction. Lift your dreams and disappointment up to God in prayer and keep on moving forward. Let your Savior's love, love that died for you, anchor you.

Then keep on dreaming! God gave you this life and walks alongside you, ready to fill your journey with joy!

That you are here—that
life exists, and identity;
That the powerful play goes on,
and you will contribute a verse.
—Walt Whitman

Now all glory to God, who is able,
through his mighty power at work within us,
to accomplish infinitely more than we might ask or think.
Glory to him in the church and in Christ Jesus
through all generations forever and ever! Amen.
Ephesians 3:20–21

Forward

It's time to go, and you are ready! Yes, you are! Your family, your school, and the life you have experienced thus far have given you the tools you need to take your next step. The faith the Holy Spirit has planted in your heart may feel a bit wobbly. But God's Word is not shaky or uncertain. It is strong and sure, and so is your heavenly Father's unconditional love.

The Lord is calling you forward. You may not know what lies ahead, but you do know that he will walk beside you always.

The past and your memories of it have shaped who you are. Many adventures lie ahead, waiting for you. So journey on, in the knowledge of Jesus Christ, who loves you and died for you! He is your best and eternal Friend. He always wants the best *for* you. He always sees the best *in* you. So go gladly, and in peace!

> *Now may our Lord Jesus Christ himself and God our Father,*
> *who loved us and by his grace*
> *gave us eternal comfort and a wonderful hope,*
> *comfort you and strengthen you*
> *in every good thing you do and say.*
> 2 Thessalonians 2:16–17

Go:

a) To depart from one place or phase; and
b) to move in faith toward another.

I heard the Lord asking,
"Whom should I send as a messenger to this people?
Who will go for us?"
I said, "Here I am. Send me."
Isaiah 6:8

I am with you always, even to the end of the age.
Matthew 28:20

To see all of CTA's books or request a catalog, visit us at www.CTAinc.com.

If this book has made a difference in your life or if you have simply enjoyed it, we would like to hear from you. Your words will encourage us! If you have suggestions for us to consider as we create books like this in the future, please send those, too.

We invite you to post your comments at https://www.facebook.com/CTAinc

Or you can reach us by e-mail at editor@CTAinc.com.
Please include the subject line: JNY5HC

You can also contact us at:

Editorial Coordinator
Department JNY5HC
CTA, Inc.
P.O. Box 1205
Fenton, MO 63026-1205